Blueprint for Cleaning Business Success: Crafting the Perfect Plan

Table of Contents

Chapter 1: Introduction to the Cleaning Business Industry

Chapter 2: Laying the Groundwork for Your Cleaning Business

Chapter 3: Identifying Your Niche and Target Audience

Chapter 4: Crafting a Business Plan for Success

Chapter 5: Legal and Administrative Essentials

Chapter 6: Branding and Marketing Strategies

Chapter 7: Building and Managing Your Team

Chapter 8: Operational Framework and Efficiency

Chapter 9: Client Acquisition and Retention Strategies

Chapter 10: Financial Management and Growth Planning

Chapter 11: Expanding and Scaling Your Business

Chapter 12: Leveraging Technology in Your Cleaning Business

Chapter 13: Navigating Challenges and Risks

Chapter 14: Case Studies and Real-World Success Stories

Chapter 15: Sustained Success and Future Trends

Chapter 1: Introduction to the Cleaning Business Industry

Detailed Overview of the Industry The cleaning business industry is a vibrant and essential sector that caters to diverse markets, including residential, commercial, and specialty cleaning services. Its resilience, even in economic downturns, highlights the steady demand for professional cleaning services. This chapter delves into the significance of the industry, its economic impact, and why it continues to attract entrepreneurs worldwide.

The cleaning industry's growth is fueled by changing lifestyles, increased awareness of hygiene, and the rise of dual-income households. As a result, individuals and businesses are increasingly outsourcing their cleaning needs. For aspiring entrepreneurs, this translates into a wealth of opportunities to carve out a niche and build a thriving business.

Introduction to the Cleaning Business Industry - Subsection 1: The Economic and Social Importance of Cleaning Services

1.1 The Role of Cleaning Businesses in Society Cleaning businesses play a critical role in maintaining public health and safety. Proper cleaning and sanitation prevent the spread of diseases, create healthier living and working environments, and contribute to overall well-being. From homes to hospitals and offices, the impact of professional cleaning services is undeniable.

1.2 The Economic Contributions of the Cleaning Industry The cleaning industry is a significant contributor to global and local economies. It generates billions of dollars annually and provides millions of jobs, ranging from entry-level positions to managerial roles. For small business owners, the cleaning industry offers a lucrative entry point with relatively low startup costs and high growth potential.

1.3 Trends Shaping the Cleaning Industry Modern trends, such as eco-friendly cleaning practices and the use of advanced technology, are reshaping the industry. Green cleaning, in particular, has gained popularity as consumers become more environmentally conscious. Entrepreneurs who embrace these trends position themselves as forward-thinking and customer-focused.

Introduction to the Cleaning Business Industry - Subsection 2: Opportunities and Challenges for Entrepreneurs

2.1 Opportunities in the Cleaning Industry

- **Low Barrier to Entry**: Unlike many industries, starting a cleaning business does not require extensive technical expertise or significant capital investment. This accessibility makes it an attractive option for first-time entrepreneurs.
- **Scalability**: Cleaning businesses can start small and grow over time. Whether you're beginning as a solo operator or with a small team, there are numerous paths to expansion, such as adding new services or targeting larger contracts.
- **Consistent Demand**: Cleaning services are always in demand, regardless of economic conditions. Essential sectors, such as healthcare and education, rely heavily on professional cleaning, ensuring a steady stream of clients.

2.2 Challenges Faced by Cleaning Business Owners

- **Competition**: The low barrier to entry also means high competition. Entrepreneurs must differentiate their services to stand out.
- **Labor Management**: Hiring and retaining reliable staff can be a challenge, especially in a high-turnover industry.

- **Operational Efficiency**: Managing schedules, supplies, and client relationships requires strong organizational skills and the adoption of efficient processes.

Introduction to the Cleaning Business Industry - Subsection 3: Key Factors for Success

3.1 Understanding Your Market Successful cleaning business owners invest time in understanding their target market. This includes identifying the specific needs of their clients and tailoring services to meet those needs. Market research is a critical first step in this process.

3.2 Delivering Quality Service The foundation of any successful cleaning business is exceptional service. Consistently exceeding client expectations builds trust, fosters loyalty, and generates positive word-of-mouth referrals. Entrepreneurs should prioritize training their staff and maintaining high-quality standards.

3.3 Building a Strong Brand A compelling brand identity sets a cleaning business apart from competitors. This includes a professional logo, a memorable tagline, and a consistent online presence. Branding is not just about aesthetics; it reflects the values and promises of your business.

3.4 Adapting to Change The cleaning industry is dynamic, with evolving client preferences and technological advancements. Staying adaptable and open to innovation is crucial for long-term success. For example, adopting eco-friendly products or leveraging digital tools can give businesses a competitive edge.

Conclusion of Chapter 1 This chapter has outlined the foundational aspects of the cleaning business industry, including its economic and social importance, opportunities and challenges, and the key factors that contribute to success. Aspiring entrepreneurs should view this industry not just as a service sector but as a platform for innovation and growth. By understanding the landscape and preparing for its demands, you're setting the stage for a thriving and rewarding business venture.

Chapter 2: Laying the Groundwork for Your Cleaning Business

Introduction

Establishing a successful cleaning business requires more than just enthusiasm and basic equipment. It demands meticulous planning, strategic decision-making, and a clear understanding of the market. This chapter delves into the essential steps to lay a solid foundation for your cleaning business. With actionable strategies, real-world examples, and step-by-step guidance, this chapter ensures you are well-equipped to navigate the challenges of the cleaning industry.

Section 1: Developing Your Vision and Mission

A compelling vision and mission serve as the compass for your cleaning business. This section explains how to craft a mission statement that resonates with your target market and reflects your core values.

- **Identifying Your Niche**
  Determine whether you want to focus on residential cleaning, commercial spaces, or specialized services like post-construction clean-ups.
  Example: "We specialize in eco-friendly residential cleaning for families who value sustainability."
- **Setting SMART Goals**
  Your goals should be Specific, Measurable, Achievable, Relevant, and Time-bound.
  Example: "Achieve a client retention rate of 90% within the first year by delivering exceptional service."
- **Understanding Your Why**
  What inspired you to start a cleaning business? A personal story or motivation can fuel your passion and help you

connect with customers.
Example: "I saw how busy families struggled to maintain clean homes and wanted to provide them with peace of mind."

Section 2: Conducting Market Research

Understanding your market is key to positioning your cleaning business for success. This section breaks down the process into manageable steps.

- **Analyzing Your Competition**
  Study local competitors to identify gaps in their services.
  Tip: Use reviews on platforms like Yelp or Google to understand what customers love and what's missing.
- **Defining Your Target Audience**
  Who are your ideal customers? Consider factors like demographics, location, and pain points.
  Example: "Our primary audience is working professionals in urban areas who need reliable weekly cleaning services."
- **Identifying Trends in the Cleaning Industry**
  Stay ahead of trends such as green cleaning, use of technology, and demand for personalized services.
  Example: "Offering app-based scheduling and eco-friendly products sets us apart in a competitive market."

Section 3: Building Your Brand

Your brand is more than a logo—it's the promise you make to your customers. This section provides a step-by-step guide to building a brand that stands out.

- **Creating a Memorable Name and Logo**
  Choose a name that is easy to remember and reflects your services. Work with a professional designer to develop a logo

that conveys professionalism.
Example: "SparkClean Solutions—brightening your spaces with every visit."
- **Developing a Unique Selling Proposition (USP)**
What makes your cleaning business unique? Highlight your strengths to attract customers.
Example: "We offer 24-hour satisfaction guarantees and flexible scheduling tailored to busy lifestyles."
- **Establishing an Online Presence**
A strong online presence is essential in today's market.
    - Create a user-friendly website with service descriptions, pricing, and testimonials.
    - Leverage social media platforms like Instagram and Facebook to showcase before-and-after photos.
    - Encourage satisfied customers to leave reviews on Google and Yelp.

Section 4: Setting Up Your Operations

Efficient operations are the backbone of a successful cleaning business. This section provides actionable advice on creating a streamlined workflow.

- **Purchasing the Right Equipment and Supplies**
Invest in high-quality equipment and cleaning products to ensure excellent results.
Example: "Using HEPA-filter vacuums and eco-friendly cleaning solutions sets us apart as a green cleaning company."
- **Hiring and Training Staff**
Your team represents your brand. Recruit employees who align with your values and provide them with comprehensive training.
Tip: Create a detailed employee handbook outlining expectations, procedures, and safety protocols.

- **Establishing Standard Operating Procedures (SOPs)**
  Document every process, from client onboarding to job completion, to ensure consistency and efficiency.

Section 5: Legal and Financial Foundations

Navigating the legal and financial aspects of your business can be daunting, but this section simplifies the process.

- **Choosing the Right Business Structure**
  Decide between a sole proprietorship, LLC, or corporation based on your goals and liability concerns.
  Tip: Consult with a business attorney to ensure you choose the best option for your needs.
- **Securing Licenses and Insurance**
  Research local regulations to obtain the necessary licenses and permits. Invest in liability insurance to protect your business.
  Example: "General liability insurance can safeguard your business against unexpected damages or accidents."
- **Setting Up Financial Systems**
  Open a separate business bank account, invest in accounting software, and track all expenses to maintain financial clarity.

Conclusion of chapter 2

The foundation you lay today determines the success of your cleaning business tomorrow. By following the steps outlined in this chapter, you'll be well on your way to building a thriving enterprise that stands out in the competitive cleaning industry.

Chapter 3: Identifying Your Niche and Target Audience

Introduction

One of the most critical steps in building a successful cleaning business is identifying your niche and understanding your target audience. Without a clear focus, you risk spreading your efforts too thin and failing to connect with the right customers. This chapter provides actionable strategies and detailed explanations to help you define your niche, pinpoint your ideal customers, and tailor your services to meet their needs.

Section 1: Understanding the Importance of Niches

A niche is a specific segment of the market where your cleaning business can excel. Establishing a niche allows you to specialize in services that meet the unique needs of a particular audience. This section highlights why choosing a niche is essential and how it can set you apart from competitors.

- **Why Specialization Matters**
  Specializing in a niche helps you build expertise, stand out in a crowded market, and attract loyal customers.
  Example: "A cleaning business specializing in eco-friendly services will appeal to environmentally conscious clients who value sustainability."
- **Exploring Different Niches in the Cleaning Industry**
  Consider the various niches available:
  - **Residential Cleaning**: Ideal for households needing regular or deep cleaning.
  - **Commercial Cleaning**: Offices and businesses requiring routine maintenance.

- o **Specialized Services**: Post-construction clean-up, move-in/move-out cleaning, or hoarding cleanup.
- o **Eco-Friendly Cleaning**: Using green products for health-conscious and environmentally aware customers.
- **Case Study: Success Through Specialization**
A Startup focusing exclusively on vacation rental cleaning grew its business by partnering with property managers, offering tailored packages, and guaranteeing fast turnaround times.

Section 2: Identifying Your Ideal Target Audience

Your target audience consists of the people or businesses most likely to benefit from your services. This section breaks down how to define and understand your ideal customers.

- **Demographics: Who Are They?**
Identify key details about your target audience, such as age, income level, location, and lifestyle.
Example: "A cleaning service for young professionals in urban areas should emphasize convenience and time-saving solutions."
- **Pain Points: What Do They Need?**
Understand the challenges your audience faces and how your services can solve them.
Example: "Busy parents may struggle to keep their homes tidy, while small business owners may need professional cleaning to create a welcoming space for customers."
- **Behavioral Insights: How Do They Choose Services?**
Analyze how potential clients search for and select cleaning businesses.
Tip: Customers often rely on online reviews, social media presence, and word-of-mouth recommendations. Make these a priority.
- **Developing Customer Profiles**
Create detailed profiles of your ideal clients to guide your

marketing and service offerings.
Example:
- **Residential Client Profile**: A dual-income family with children, living in the suburbs, seeking bi-weekly cleaning to save time.
- **Commercial Client Profile**: A small law firm in need of weekly after-hours cleaning to maintain a professional appearance.

Section 3: Tailoring Your Services to Your Niche and Audience

Once you've identified your niche and audience, it's time to align your services with their expectations. This section explains how to customize your offerings to create maximum impact.

- **Developing a Service Menu**
  Create a clear and comprehensive list of services tailored to your niche.
  Example:
    - For residential cleaning: deep cleaning, regular upkeep, and one-time services like spring cleaning.
    - For eco-friendly niches: use of biodegradable products and allergen-free solutions.
- **Setting Competitive Pricing**
  Price your services based on market research, client expectations, and the value you provide.
  Tip: Offer tiered packages (e.g., basic, standard, and premium) to cater to different budgets.
  Example: "Basic package includes surface cleaning, while premium adds carpet steaming and window washing."
- **Delivering Exceptional Customer Experience**
  Build trust and loyalty by exceeding expectations.
    - Respond promptly to inquiries and feedback.
    - Personalize your services to meet specific client needs.
    - Follow up after a service to ensure satisfaction.
- **Utilizing Technology for Efficiency**
  Leverage technology to improve operations and enhance the client experience.

Example: "Offer online booking and automated reminders to make scheduling easy for busy clients."

Section 4: Marketing to Your Target Audience

Reaching the right audience requires a well-thought-out marketing plan. This section provides strategies to connect with your ideal clients effectively.

- **Building a Strong Online Presence**
    - Create a professional website showcasing your services, pricing, and testimonials.
    - Use social media platforms like Instagram and TikTok to share before-and-after photos, cleaning tips, and client success stories.
- **Investing in Local Advertising**
  Focus on your local community to build a loyal customer base.
  Example: "Distribute flyers in neighborhoods, advertise in local directories, and attend community events."
- **Encouraging Referrals and Reviews**
  Happy clients can be your best marketers.
  Tip: Offer referral discounts to existing clients who bring in new business.
  Example: "Get 10% off your next cleaning service for every referral that books with us."
- **Networking with Complementary Businesses**
  Partner with real estate agents, property managers, and home improvement companies to expand your reach.

Section 5: Measuring Success and Adjusting Your Approach

Your niche and target audience may evolve over time, so it's important to track your progress and adapt as needed. This section explains how to monitor your success and refine your strategy.

- **Tracking Key Metrics**
  Monitor important metrics such as customer acquisition costs, client retention rates, and average revenue per client.
  Example: "A high retention rate indicates that your services and customer experience are meeting expectations."
- **Gathering Customer Feedback**
  Regularly ask for feedback to identify areas for improvement.
  Example: "Use surveys or follow-up emails to learn what clients appreciate and what they'd like to see improved."
- **Adapting to Market Trends**
  Stay informed about changes in the cleaning industry, such as demand for new services or innovations in cleaning technology.
- **Expanding or Pivoting Your Niche**
  Once you've established a strong presence in your initial niche, consider expanding into complementary services.
  Example: "A residential cleaning business might add carpet shampooing or organizing services."

Conclusion

Identifying your niche and target audience is the cornerstone of a thriving cleaning business. By understanding who your ideal clients are and aligning your services with their needs, you position your business for long-term success. The insights and strategies in this chapter will not only help you attract the right customers but also ensure your cleaning business stands out as a leader in the industry.

Chapter 4: Crafting a Business Plan for Success

Introduction

A well-crafted business plan is the foundation of a successful cleaning business. It provides a roadmap, helps secure funding, and ensures clarity in operations and growth strategies. In this chapter, we break down the key elements of a business plan and guide you step-by-step to create a winning plan tailored to your cleaning business.

Section 1: The Essential Components of a Business Plan

To create an effective business plan, it's important to understand its key components and how each contributes to your success.

- **Executive Summary**
  This is the first section but should be written last. It provides a snapshot of your business plan, highlighting the key points.
    - What it should include:
        - Business name, location, and mission statement.
        - Overview of your services and target audience.
        - A brief outline of your financial goals and growth projections.
        Example:
        "[Your Business Name] is a professional cleaning company specializing in eco-friendly residential and commercial cleaning solutions. Based in [Your City], we aim to provide exceptional service to environmentally conscious clients while promoting healthier spaces."
- **Company Description**
  Provide details about your business, including its legal structure, mission, and what sets it apart.
  Example:

- Legal structure: Sole proprietorship, LLC, or corporation.
- Unique selling proposition: "We use non-toxic, biodegradable cleaning products and offer a satisfaction guarantee."

- **Market Analysis**

  Analyze your niche and target audience to showcase your understanding of the market.
  - Include:
    - Industry trends: "The demand for green cleaning services is growing by 15% annually."
    - Competitor analysis: Highlight gaps in services your competitors provide.
    - Target audience profile: "Our primary clients are dual-income families and small businesses in urban areas."

- **Service Offering**

  Clearly describe the services your cleaning business will provide.
  Example:
  - Basic services: General cleaning, dusting, vacuuming.
  - Premium services: Carpet cleaning, window washing, post-construction clean-ups.

- **Marketing and Sales Strategy**

  Outline how you will attract and retain customers.
  Example:
  - Digital marketing plan: Use social media ads, SEO for your website, and customer testimonials.
  - Referral programs: Reward loyal clients for referrals.
  - Partnerships: Collaborate with real estate agents and property managers.

Section 2: Crafting Financial Projections and Budget Plans

The financial section of your business plan helps determine the viability of your cleaning business and attracts investors or lenders.

- **Startup Costs**
  List the initial expenses required to launch your business.
  Example:
    - Equipment and supplies: Vacuums, mops, cleaning products.
    - Marketing: Website creation, business cards, and initial advertising.
    - Legal and administrative fees: Business registration, permits, and insurance.
- **Revenue Projections**
  Estimate your income based on services offered, pricing, and expected client volume.
  Example:
    - If you charge $100 per cleaning session and serve 10 clients weekly, your weekly revenue will be $1,000.
- **Break-even Analysis**
  Determine when your business will start making a profit.
  Example:
    - Calculate fixed costs (e.g., rent, utilities) and variable costs (e.g., supplies, labor).
    - Identify the number of clients you need to cover these costs.
- **Ongoing Operating Budget**
  Create a monthly budget to manage cash flow and track expenses.
  Example:
    - Allocate funds for employee wages, equipment maintenance, and marketing campaigns.
- **Funding Requirements (If Applicable)**
  If you need financial assistance, specify the amount and how it will be used.
  Example: "We require $20,000 in Startup capital to cover initial equipment purchases, marketing, and working capital for the first three months."

Section 3: Creating an Operational Plan

The operational plan outlines how your cleaning business will function day-to-day.

- **Service Workflow**
  Design a step-by-step process for delivering services to ensure consistency.
  Example:
    1. Initial client consultation and scheduling.
    2. On-site cleaning following a standardized checklist.
    3. Follow-up communication to ensure client satisfaction.
- **Staffing Plan**
  Outline how many employees you'll need, their roles, and training plans.
  Example:

    - Role: Cleaning technicians.
    - Training: Provide instruction on using cleaning equipment, safety protocols, and customer service.

- **Technology and Tools**
  Invest in tools to streamline operations and improve efficiency.
  Example:

    - Scheduling software for booking appointments.
    - Payment platforms for seamless transactions.

- **Quality Control**
  Develop a system for monitoring service quality and addressing issues.
  Example:

    - Conduct random service audits.
    - Use customer feedback forms to identify areas for improvement.

Section 4: Risk Assessment and Contingency Plans

Every business faces risks, but planning ahead minimizes their impact.

- **Identifying Risks**
  Highlight potential challenges, such as:
    - High competition in your area.
    - Rising costs of supplies.
    - Employee turnover.
- **Mitigation Strategies**
  Outline how you'll address these risks.
  Example:
    - Diversify services to differentiate your business.
    - Build relationships with suppliers to negotiate better deals.
    - Offer employee incentives to reduce turnover.
- **Emergency Planning**
  Prepare for unexpected events like equipment breakdowns or economic downturns.
  Example: Maintain a reserve fund to cover unforeseen expenses.

Section 5: Reviewing and Updating Your Business Plan

A business plan isn't static—it evolves as your business grows.

- **Regular Reviews**
  Schedule quarterly reviews to evaluate your progress and make necessary adjustments.
- **Incorporating Feedback**
  Use insights from clients, employees, and financial reports to refine your strategies.
- **Scaling Your Business**
  Identify opportunities for expansion, such as offering new services or entering new markets.

Conclusion

Crafting a detailed business plan is essential for launching and growing a successful cleaning business. By clearly defining your goals, strategies, and operational processes, you set yourself up for long-term success. Use the steps outlined in this chapter to create a plan that not only guides your business but also impresses potential investors and partners.

Chapter 5: Legal and Administrative Essentials

Introduction

Starting a cleaning business requires more than just a passion for providing excellent services. To operate legally and professionally, you must address essential legal and administrative requirements. This chapter guides you through the necessary steps to ensure your business complies with regulations, operates smoothly, and builds trust with clients. Whether you're a solo entrepreneur or building a team, these fundamentals will help you establish a solid foundation.

Section 1: Legalizing Your Cleaning Business

1.1 Choosing a Legal Structure

Your business's legal structure determines its taxation, liability, and day-to-day operations. Here are the common options:

- **Sole Proprietorship**:
    - Ideal for solo entrepreneurs.
    - Simple and affordable to set up.
    - Drawback: You are personally liable for business debts.
- **Limited Liability Company (LLC)**:
    - Protects your personal assets from business liabilities.
    - Flexible in terms of taxation.
    - Slightly more paperwork compared to a sole proprietorship.
- **Corporation**:
    - Suitable for larger businesses or those seeking investors.
    - Requires detailed record-keeping and higher costs. *Tip*: For most cleaning startups, an LLC strikes a balance between simplicity and liability protection.

1.2 Registering Your Business Name

Choose a name that reflects your brand and stands out in the market. Ensure it's:

- Memorable and professional (e.g., "Eco-Clean Solutions").
- Not already in use; check your local government's business registry or use online databases.

1.3 Obtaining Business Licenses and Permits

Many jurisdictions require cleaning businesses to have specific licenses or permits.

- Check local, state, or national regulations.
- Examples:
    - General business license.

- Home occupation permit (if running the business from home).
- Environmental permits for businesses using chemicals.

1.4 Meeting Insurance Requirements

Insurance protects your business and reassures clients. Common types include:

- **General Liability Insurance**: Covers accidental damages (e.g., spilling cleaning products on expensive furniture).
- **Workers' Compensation Insurance**: Required if you hire employees; covers workplace injuries.
- **Bonding Insurance**: Increases client trust by covering theft or dishonesty claims.
  Pro Tip: Present proof of insurance to clients as part of your professionalism.

Section 2: Administrative Foundations for Smooth Operations

2.1 Setting Up a Business Bank Account

Separating personal and business finances is essential for:

- Clear bookkeeping.
- Easier tax filing.
- Enhanced professionalism (clients pay your business, not you personally).
  Tip: Choose a bank offering perks like free monthly statements or small business support.

2.2 Record-Keeping and Accounting

Good financial records are crucial for tracking growth, filing taxes, and attracting investors.

- Use software like QuickBooks or Wave for:
  - Invoicing clients.

- - Tracking expenses and revenue.
  - Monitoring payroll (if you have employees).
- Keep receipts for equipment purchases, marketing, and transportation costs.

2.3 Creating Service Contracts

Written contracts clarify expectations and reduce disputes. Include:

- A detailed list of services offered.
- Payment terms (e.g., upfront payment, installment options).
- Cancellation and refund policies.
  Example: "Clients must cancel within 24 hours to avoid a cancellation fee of $25."

2.4 Setting Up Communication Systems

Efficient communication ensures client satisfaction and operational efficiency.

- Use a dedicated phone line or business email.
- Consider customer relationship management (CRM) software to:
  - Schedule services.
  - Send reminders.
  - Manage client feedback.

Section 3: Compliance, Taxes, and Growth Strategies

3.1 Understanding Your Tax Obligations

Taxes vary based on your legal structure and location.

- Common requirements include:
  - Income tax (based on your profits).
  - Sales tax (if applicable to cleaning services in your area).
  - Employment tax (if you hire workers).

- Work with a tax professional to avoid penalties and maximize deductions.
  Deduction Tip: Claim expenses for cleaning supplies, uniforms, vehicle mileage, and marketing.

3.2 Employment Laws and Hiring Policies

If your cleaning business involves a team, ensure compliance with employment laws.

- Understand minimum wage and overtime regulations.
- Provide proper training on safety measures, such as handling cleaning chemicals.
- Use employment contracts detailing job roles, pay rates, and expectations.

3.3 Protecting Client Data

Clients entrust you with access to their homes or businesses. Build their trust by safeguarding their information.

- Use secure systems for storing client addresses, payment details, and service history.
- Train employees on confidentiality policies.

3.4 Scaling Your Business Legally

As your business grows, revisit your legal and administrative setup:

- Upgrade licenses if offering new services (e.g., floor polishing, upholstery cleaning).
- Adjust insurance coverage to match your expanded operations.
- Create an employee handbook for consistent team management.

Section 4: Real-World Application

To bring these concepts to life, let's look at an example of a cleaning business starting from scratch:

Case Study: CleanBright LLC

- **Startup Phase**:
  CleanBright LLC began as a two-person operation in [City]. The owner, Sarah, registered her business as an LLC, purchased general liability insurance, and opened a business account.
- **Administrative Setup**:
  Sarah used accounting software to track expenses and created a simple yet professional service contract for clients.
- **Growth Phase**:
  After six months, CleanBright expanded by hiring two part-time cleaners. Sarah ensured compliance with employment laws and offered basic training on handling cleaning tools.

Outcome: Sarah's meticulous attention to legal and administrative details helped CleanBright earn client trust and scale sustainably.

Conclusion

Understanding and implementing the legal and administrative essentials of your cleaning business ensures that your operations run smoothly, your clients trust you, and your business grows confidently. These foundational steps may seem complex, but they're investments in your long-term success. Follow the guidelines in this chapter to build a compliant, professional, and scalable cleaning business that stands out in the industry.

Chapter 6: Branding and Marketing Strategies

Introduction

In the competitive cleaning industry, standing out is critical. Branding and marketing strategies are your tools to attract clients, retain them, and grow your business sustainably. This chapter simplifies these concepts into actionable steps, helping you create a strong identity and implement marketing tactics that resonate with your target audience. Whether you're starting small or planning big, these strategies will position your cleaning business as a trusted, professional, and sought-after brand.

Section 1: Crafting a Memorable Brand Identity

1.1 Understanding Your Brand

Your brand is more than just a logo or tagline—it's the perception people have of your business. For a cleaning business, this means reliability, professionalism, and excellence in service.

- **Core Elements of a Strong Brand**:
    - **Name**: Choose a name that's memorable, easy to pronounce, and conveys professionalism.
      Example: *SparklePro Cleaning Services* suggests expertise and quality.
    - **Logo**: Invest in a clean, modern design that reflects your services (e.g., brooms, sparkling windows).
    - **Tagline**: Create a short, impactful tagline like *"Making Every Space Shine"*.

1.2 Defining Your Unique Selling Proposition (USP)

Your USP differentiates you from competitors. Identify what makes your cleaning business special:

- Eco-friendly products?

- Guaranteed satisfaction?
- Specialized services like post-construction cleanup?
Example: "We use non-toxic, eco-friendly cleaners for a healthier home and planet."

1.3 Building Trust Through Branding

A trustworthy brand attracts loyal customers. Consider:

- Professional uniforms for staff.
- Well-branded cleaning vehicles.
- Clear communication in all client interactions.

Section 2: Implementing Effective Marketing Strategies

2.1 Leveraging Online Platforms

Most potential clients start their search online. Establishing a strong digital presence is non-negotiable.

- **Website Essentials**:
    - Include your services, pricing, contact information, and customer reviews.
    - Optimize for mobile use since many clients search via smartphones.
    - Add booking functionality to simplify scheduling.
- **Search Engine Optimization (SEO)**:
    - Use keywords like "residential cleaning services," "office cleaning near me," and "affordable cleaners" on your site.
    - Write blog posts about cleaning tips or "how to choose the best cleaning service."

2.2 Social Media Marketing

Social platforms are excellent for engaging with your audience.

- Use Facebook and Instagram to post:

- Before-and-after photos of your cleaning work.
- Client testimonials and success stories.
- Cleaning hacks or tips (e.g., "How to Remove Stubborn Carpet Stains").
- Create engaging videos for TikTok or YouTube showcasing your team in action or tutorials for small cleaning tasks.

2.3 Traditional Marketing Techniques

While digital marketing is crucial, traditional methods still work for local cleaning businesses.

- **Flyers and Posters**: Distribute in residential neighborhoods, gyms, daycare centers, and coffee shops.
- **Business Cards:** Hand them out after every service and at networking events.
- **Vehicle Branding**: Turn your car into a moving billboard with your business name, logo, and contact info.

2.4 Partnering with Local Businesses

Collaborate with complementary businesses such as real estate agencies, moving companies, or property managers.

- Offer referral discounts or joint promotional deals.
  Example: "Book with us and receive 10% off your next moving service!"

Section 3: Building a Loyal Customer Base

3.1 Creating an Exceptional Customer Experience

Satisfied clients are your best marketers. Focus on:

- Timely communication (e.g., confirmation messages for bookings).
- Exceeding expectations with thorough, detailed cleaning.
- Offering follow-up surveys to gather feedback.

3.2 Referral Programs

Encourage clients to refer friends and family by offering incentives:

- Discounts on future services.
- Free add-ons like window cleaning or carpet shampooing.
  Example: "Refer a friend and get 20% off your next service!"

3.3 Loyalty Programs

Reward repeat customers to ensure long-term relationships.

- Offer a free cleaning after a certain number of paid services.
- Provide holiday discounts or surprise bonuses (e.g., free oven cleaning during the festive season).

3.4 Showcasing Client Testimonials

Word-of-mouth remains a powerful tool. Use positive reviews to build credibility:

- Post them on your website and social media.
- Create video testimonials for more authenticity.
- Encourage satisfied clients to leave reviews on Google and Yelp.

Section 4: Monitoring and Adjusting Your Strategies

4.1 Tracking Marketing Success

Measure the effectiveness of your efforts to maximize ROI:

- Use analytics tools to track website traffic and social media engagement.
- Ask clients how they heard about your services (e.g., referral, flyer, Google).

- Test different strategies and focus on those delivering the best results.

4.2 Adapting to Market Trends

Stay ahead by adjusting to changes in customer needs and preferences.

- If eco-friendly cleaning is trending, expand your green cleaning services.
- Keep an eye on competitors and innovate where possible.

4.3 Budgeting for Marketing

Allocate a percentage of your earnings to reinvest in marketing.

- Start with low-cost methods like social media and gradually add paid ads as your business grows.

Real-World Example: Brand Success Story

Case Study: FreshStart Cleaning Co.

- **Challenge**: Starting from scratch in a crowded urban market.
- **Solution**:
    - Created a memorable brand with a logo featuring green leaves to symbolize eco-friendliness.
    - Used Facebook to post weekly cleaning tips, boosting engagement.
    - Partnered with local moving companies to offer bundled discounts.
- **Outcome**: Within a year, FreshStart became a go-to name for busy families seeking reliable and eco-conscious cleaning services.

Conclusion

Building a strong brand and implementing effective marketing strategies are critical to your cleaning business's success. These tactics will not only help you attract clients but also retain them and grow your presence in the competitive market. With dedication, creativity, and consistent effort, you'll position your business as a trusted leader in the cleaning industry.

Chapter 7: Building and Managing Your Team

Introduction

No business succeeds without a strong, reliable team—and the cleaning industry is no exception. Your team is the backbone of your operations, and their performance will shape your company's reputation and growth. This chapter provides a step-by-step guide to hiring, training, and managing your team effectively, ensuring your cleaning business thrives.

Section 1: Hiring the Right Team

1.1 Identifying Roles and Responsibilities

Before hiring, clarify the roles you need to fill. In a cleaning business, the following positions are crucial:

- **Cleaners/Technicians**: The frontline workers responsible for delivering exceptional cleaning services.
- **Supervisors**: Oversee quality control and manage the team during larger jobs.
- **Administrative Staff**: Handle scheduling, billing, and customer inquiries.

For small businesses, these roles may overlap. As your business grows, specialized positions become essential.

1.2 Crafting a Job Description

An attractive and clear job description will draw the right candidates. Include:

- **Title**: E.g., *Residential Cleaning Technician* or *Commercial Cleaning Specialist*.
- **Duties**: List responsibilities like cleaning, restocking supplies, and following safety protocols.

- **Requirements**: Detail any needed skills (e.g., attention to detail, ability to lift 20 pounds) or certifications (e.g., OSHA compliance).
- **Benefits**: Mention perks like flexible schedules, growth opportunities, or performance bonuses.

1.3 Where to Find Candidates

Post your job listing on:

- Local job boards or community boards.
- Social media platforms like Facebook groups or LinkedIn.
- Online job platforms like Indeed or ZipRecruiter.
  Referrals from trusted friends, family, or colleagues can also be a goldmine.

1.4 Screening and Interviewing

Choose candidates who align with your values of professionalism, reliability, and customer satisfaction. During interviews:

- Ask about their cleaning experience and problem-solving skills.
- Use situational questions like, "How would you handle a dissatisfied customer?"
- Assess their soft skills: Are they friendly, punctual, and team-oriented?

1.5 Conducting Background Checks

Your team will work in clients' homes and offices, so trust is paramount. Verify:

- Employment history.
- References from previous employers.
- Criminal background checks, if necessary.

Section 2: Training and Onboarding

2.1 Importance of a Thorough Onboarding Process

Proper onboarding sets the tone for success. It helps employees understand your expectations, processes, and company culture.

2.2 Designing an Effective Training Program

- **Orientation**: Introduce your business's mission, vision, and values.
- **Skill Training**: Teach cleaning techniques, use of equipment, and safety procedures.
- **Customer Interaction**: Train employees to communicate professionally with clients.
  Example: Role-play scenarios like addressing client complaints or offering additional services.

2.3 Providing a Training Checklist

Create a checklist to ensure consistency across employees. Include:

- Proper handling of cleaning supplies.
- Time management for efficient service delivery.
- Understanding and adhering to eco-friendly or specialty cleaning procedures.

2.4 Encouraging Continuous Learning

Offer opportunities for skill development through:

- Workshops on advanced cleaning techniques (e.g., carpet restoration, upholstery cleaning).
- Certifications like Green Cleaning Technician or Commercial Cleaning Specialist.

Section 3: Managing and Retaining Your Team

3.1 Establishing a Positive Work Environment

A happy team is a productive team. Foster a supportive environment by:

- Treating employees with respect and fairness.
- Providing regular breaks and reasonable workloads.
- Encouraging teamwork and open communication.

3.2 Setting Clear Expectations

Define what success looks like in your company.

- Set performance standards for quality and efficiency.
- Provide written policies on attendance, dress code, and workplace behavior.
- Regularly review these expectations during team meetings or performance evaluations.

3.3 Motivating and Rewarding Your Team

Recognize and reward hard work to maintain morale and loyalty.

- Offer bonuses for excellent performance or customer feedback.
- Create an *Employee of the Month* program.
- Provide small perks, like gift cards or paid time off, as incentives.

3.4 Communication Is Key

Maintain open lines of communication to address concerns and provide feedback. Use:

- Regular team meetings to discuss goals, challenges, and achievements.
- One-on-one sessions for individual feedback and growth opportunities.

- Anonymous suggestion boxes to gather honest input from employees.

3.5 Conflict Resolution

Conflicts may arise in any team. Address them promptly and professionally by:

- Listening to all parties involved.
- Mediating disputes and finding fair solutions.
- Reinforcing your company's code of conduct.

Section 4: Scaling Your Team

4.1 Knowing When to Expand

Growth often requires additional staff. Signs it's time to scale include:

- Increasing demand for your services.
- Overburdened employees or consistent overtime hours.
- Clients requesting new services outside your current capacity.

4.2 Building Leadership Roles

As your team grows, develop leaders within your workforce. Promote from within to:

- Boost employee morale and loyalty.
- Ensure managers understand your business values and practices.

4.3 Using Technology to Manage Larger Teams

Invest in tools to streamline operations:

- Scheduling software like Jobber or Housecall Pro.

- Payroll and HR management tools like Gusto.
- Communication apps like Slack or WhatsApp for team updates.

Real-World Example: Building a High-Performing Cleaning Team

Case Study: CrystalClean Co.

- **Challenge**: Rapid business growth led to inconsistent service quality.
- **Solution**:
    - Hired a dedicated training manager to onboard new employees.
    - Established a reward system for punctuality and positive client reviews.
    - Adopted scheduling software to improve workflow.
- **Outcome**: Employee satisfaction increased, client retention improved by 30%, and operations ran more smoothly.

Conclusion

Building and managing a cleaning team requires patience, strategic planning, and continuous improvement. By hiring the right people, providing comprehensive training, and fostering a positive work environment, you'll establish a team that represents your business with excellence. Your employees are your most valuable asset—invest in them, and your business will thrive.

Chapter 8: Operational Framework and Efficiency

Introduction

Operational efficiency is the heart of a thriving cleaning business. Without a structured framework, even the most ambitious entrepreneurs can face delays, miscommunication, or financial losses. This chapter outlines how to design and implement an operational framework that maximizes efficiency, reduces overhead costs, and delivers consistent service quality to clients.

Section 1: Establishing a Robust Operational Framework

1.1 Why an Operational Framework is Vital

An operational framework serves as the blueprint for how your cleaning business functions. It ensures tasks are streamlined, responsibilities are clear, and resources are used effectively.

Key benefits include:

- Reducing waste and inefficiencies.
- Ensuring uniform service quality.
- Scaling your business seamlessly as demand grows.

1.2 Mapping Out Your Workflow

Begin by defining every step of your business operations:

1. **Client Onboarding**:
   - How will you gather client requirements?
   - Will you offer free consultations or estimates?
2. **Job Scheduling**:
   - Decide the tools or software you'll use for scheduling.
   - Create a buffer for delays or unforeseen issues.
3. **Service Delivery**:
   - Develop standard operating procedures (SOPs) for different cleaning tasks.
   - Allocate resources (supplies, equipment, and personnel) efficiently.
4. **Follow-Up**:
   - Implement feedback collection mechanisms to evaluate customer satisfaction.

1.3 Tools and Technology for Operations Management

Invest in tools that enhance operational efficiency:

- **Scheduling Software**: Platforms like Jobber or Field Puls- streamline client appointments and workforce management.
- **Inventory Management Systems**: Track cleaning supplies to avoid shortages or excess stock.
- **Time-Tracking Apps**: Monitor employees' productivity and time spent on each job.

Section 2: Enhancing Efficiency in Daily Operations

2.1 Optimizing Resource Allocation

- **Staff Management**: Match team sizes to the scale of each job. For example, a small residential cleaning may require 2 cleaners, while a large commercial property might need 6–8 cleaners.
- **Equipment Distribution**: Avoid downtime by ensuring each team has access to essential tools, such as vacuums, mops, and eco-friendly cleaning agents.

2.2 Standard Operating Procedures (SOPs)

Create detailed SOPs for every service you offer. SOPs ensure consistency and eliminate guesswork for your staff.

Example: *Deep Cleaning SOP for Kitchens*

1. Clear all countertops.
2. Use an eco-friendly degreaser on stovetops and ovens.
3. Sanitize all surfaces with a microfiber cloth.
4. Mop floors with a disinfectant solution.

2.3 Managing Time Effectively

Time management is critical for meeting client expectations and reducing operational costs.

- **Route Optimization**: Plan daily routes to minimize travel time between jobs. Apps like Google Maps or specialized logistics software can help.
- **Task Prioritization**: Assign high-priority tasks first, ensuring essential services are completed even during time crunches.

2.4 Energy Efficiency and Sustainability

Being environmentally conscious can save costs and appeal to eco-conscious clients.

- Switch to energy-efficient equipment like HEPA-filter vacuums.
- Use biodegradable cleaning products to reduce waste.
- Train employees on water conservation techniques during cleaning tasks.

Section 3: Monitoring and Improving Performance

3.1 Key Performance Indicators (KPIs)

Track these KPIs to assess and improve your operations:

- **Customer Satisfaction Score**: Gauge how happy clients are with your services.
- **Job Completion Rate**: Measure how often tasks are completed on schedule.
- **Employee Productivity**: Monitor average time spent per cleaning job.

3.2 Implementing Quality Assurance (QA) Programs

QA programs help identify and fix operational issues. Steps to build an effective QA program:

- **Regular Inspections**: Assign supervisors to evaluate completed jobs.
- **Customer Feedback**: Actively collect and analyze client reviews.
- **Training Updates**: Address identified gaps with refresher training sessions.

3.3 Addressing Operational Challenges

Be prepared to tackle common challenges:

- **Last-Minute Cancellations**: Have a cancellation policy that protects your revenue.
- **Supply Shortages**: Keep an emergency stock of essential items.
- **Staff Shortages**: Maintain a list of part-time workers who can step in during peak periods.

3.4 Continuous Improvement

Foster a culture of improvement by:

- Conducting monthly reviews of your processes.
- Gathering suggestions from employees on how to improve workflows.
- Staying updated on industry trends and adapting your practices accordingly.

Real-World Example: Operational Excellence

Case Study: Spotless Solutions LLC

- **Challenge**: Frequent delays in job completion and inconsistent service quality.
- **Solution**:
    - Introduced SOPs for each cleaning service.
    - Adopted scheduling software to automate job assignments.
    - Conducted monthly QA checks to ensure compliance with standards.
- **Outcome**:
    - Reduced average job completion time by 20%.
    - Improved customer retention rate by 35%.

Conclusion

Building a streamlined operational framework is crucial for the success of any cleaning business. By adopting efficient workflows, utilizing technology, and focusing on continuous improvement, you can enhance both productivity and client satisfaction. Operational efficiency not only sets you apart from competitors but also lays the foundation for long-term success.

Chapter 9: Client Acquisition and Retention Strategies

Introduction

In the cleaning service industry, acquiring clients is just the beginning. Building a loyal customer base is key to sustainable growth and long-term success. This chapter explores proven strategies to attract, convert, and retain clients. From leveraging digital marketing to providing exceptional customer service, these insights are designed to set your cleaning business apart.

Section 1: Effective Client Acquisition Strategies

1.1 Understanding Your Target Market

Before acquiring clients, you must understand who they are and what they need. Cleaning services often cater to:

1. **Residential Clients**: Homeowners or tenants seeking recurring cleaning services or one-time deep cleans.
2. **Commercial Clients**: Offices, retail stores, and businesses requiring janitorial services.
3. **Specialized Clients**: Clients needing niche services like carpet cleaning, post-construction cleanup, or eco-friendly cleaning.

1.2 Building an Online Presence

An online presence is non-negotiable for client acquisition. Here's how to create one that converts:

- **Professional Website**: Your website should include a detailed services page, contact form, client testimonials, and an easy-to-navigate design.
- **Search Engine Optimization (SEO)**: Use cleaning industry keywords like *"professional cleaning services near me,"* *"affordable house cleaning,"* and *"commercial janitorial services"* to rank higher in search engines.

- **Social Media Marketing**: Leverage platforms like Facebook and Instagram to share before-and-after photos, promotions, and client reviews.

1.3 Leveraging Referrals and Partnerships

- **Client Referrals**: Offer discounts or rewards to existing clients who refer new customers.
- **Real Estate Agents and Property Managers**: Partner with these professionals to provide move-in/move-out cleaning services.
- **Local Businesses**: Network with other small businesses, like home improvement stores or interior designers, for cross-promotion opportunities.

1.4 Paid Advertising

Invest in targeted advertising to reach potential clients quickly.

- **Google Ads**: Target keywords like *"professional cleaners for hire"* or *"local cleaning services."*
- **Facebook Ads**: Run campaigns targeting homeowners or businesses within a specific radius.
- **Local Directories**: List your services on platforms like Yelp, Angie's List, or Thumbtack.

Section 2: Delivering Exceptional Service for Retention

2.1 First Impressions Matter

The first interaction with a client sets the tone for the relationship. Tips for making a great impression:

- **Professional Appearance**: Ensure your team wears uniforms and presents a polished image.
- **Punctuality**: Arrive on time, equipped with all necessary supplies.

- **Attention to Detail**: Exceed expectations by addressing areas clients might overlook, like light fixtures or baseboards.

2.2 Building Trust and Reliability

Clients are more likely to stay with a service they trust.

- **Transparent Pricing**: Provide clear and upfront quotes to avoid surprises.
- **Consistent Quality**: Train your team to follow standardized cleaning protocols.
- **Communication**: Keep clients informed about any delays, changes, or updates.

2.3 Personalization and Customization

Offer personalized services to make clients feel valued.

- **Custom Cleaning Plans**: Adapt services to meet specific client needs, such as eco-friendly cleaning for families with allergies.
- **Special Occasions**: Send reminders or offer discounts for seasonal cleanings, like spring cleaning or holiday preparation.

Section 3: Strategies to Retain Clients and Build Loyalty

3.1 Rewarding Loyalty

Loyal clients are the foundation of a successful cleaning business. Implement these loyalty-building strategies:

- **Loyalty Programs**: Offer discounts, free cleanings, or gift cards for repeat customers.
- **Exclusive Perks**: Provide early access to promotions or special services.

3.2 Seeking and Acting on Feedback

Customer feedback is invaluable for retention and improvement.

- **Surveys**: Send short post-service surveys to gauge satisfaction.
- **Follow-Ups**: Check in with clients periodically to ensure their needs are being met.
- **Act Quickly**: Address any complaints or issues promptly and professionally.

3.3 Staying Top-of-Mind

Regular communication helps you stay in the forefront of clients' minds.

- **Email Marketing**: Share cleaning tips, seasonal promotions, or company updates.
- **Social Media Engagement**: Post helpful content, like DIY cleaning hacks or success stories, to engage your audience.
- **Holiday Greetings**: Send holiday cards or messages to show appreciation.

3.4 Upselling and Cross-Selling

Encourage existing clients to try additional services.

- **Bundled Packages**: Offer packages that combine multiple services, like carpet cleaning and window washing.
- **Add-On Services**: Suggest add-ons like oven cleaning, pressure washing, or organizing services.

Real-World Example: Mastering Client Retention

Case Study: Pureluxe Cleaning Services

- **Challenge**: High customer turnover due to inconsistent service quality.

- **Solution**:
    - Standardized cleaning protocols and quality checks.
    - Introduced a loyalty program offering discounts for referrals and repeat business.
    - Implemented a CRM system to track client preferences and follow-ups.
- **Outcome**:
    - Increased client retention by 50%.
    - Received consistent 5-star reviews, boosting new client inquiries.

Conclusion

Client acquisition and retention are two sides of the same coin. While effective marketing attracts clients, exceptional service keeps them coming back. By implementing the strategies outlined in this chapter, your cleaning business can stand out as a trusted and reliable provider.

Chapter 10: Financial Management and Growth Planning

Introduction

Financial management and growth planning are essential to the long-term success of your cleaning business. Proper budgeting, cost control, and strategic planning can mean the difference between thriving or struggling. This chapter provides step-by-step guidance on managing your finances, scaling operations, and preparing for sustainable growth. Whether you're just starting or aiming to expand, the principles here are tailored for the cleaning service industry and designed to empower you with confidence.

Section 1: Laying the Foundation for Financial Success

1.1 Creating a Realistic Budget

A comprehensive budget ensures you allocate resources effectively.

- **Understand Your Fixed Costs**: These include rent, insurance, equipment, and software subscriptions.
- **Identify Variable Costs**: Such as employee wages, cleaning supplies, and fuel expenses.
- **Plan for Emergencies**: Set aside a portion of your earnings for unforeseen expenses like equipment breakdowns.
- **Monitor Cash Flow**: Track your income and expenses weekly to avoid surprises.

1.2 Setting Competitive Pricing

Your pricing structure should reflect the quality of your services while remaining competitive.

- **Hourly vs. Flat Rates**: Choose based on the nature of the job. For example, charge hourly for deep cleaning and flat rates for recurring residential services.
- **Market Research**: Research competitors to gauge pricing norms in your area.
- **Value-Added Services**: Justify higher prices by offering perks like eco-friendly cleaning or loyalty rewards.
- **Profit Margins**: Aim for at least a 20%-30% margin after covering costs.

1.3 Choosing the Right Financial Tools

Managing your business finances is easier with the right tools:

- **Accounting Software**: Use platforms like QuickBooks or Wave for bookkeeping and invoicing.
- **Payroll Solutions**: Automate employee payments with services like Gusto or Paychex.
- **Expense Tracking Apps**: Simplify tracking and categorizing business expenses.

Section 2: Strategies for Financial Efficiency

2.1 Reducing Overhead Costs

Minimizing expenses without compromising quality boosts profitability.

- **Buy Supplies in Bulk**: Take advantage of wholesale pricing for cleaning supplies.
- **Energy Efficiency**: Use energy-saving appliances and LED lighting in your operations.

- **Optimize Routes**: Use route planning software to reduce fuel consumption for mobile cleaning teams.

2.2 Maximizing Revenue Streams

Diversify income sources to boost overall revenue:

- **Offer Add-On Services**: Carpet cleaning, window washing, or pressure cleaning can increase average transaction value.
- **Seasonal Promotions**: Create packages for spring cleaning, holiday preparation, or post-event cleanups.
- **Partner with Local Businesses**: Offer exclusive deals to nearby offices or residential complexes.

2.3 Monitoring Key Performance Indicators (KPIs)

Track KPIs to measure your financial health:

- **Customer Acquisition Cost (CAC)**: Calculate how much you spend to gain a new client.
- **Customer Lifetime Value (CLV)**: Measure the total revenue a client generates during their relationship with your business.
- **Profit Margins**: Keep an eye on net and gross margins to ensure sustainability.
- **Employee Efficiency**: Monitor how much revenue each team member generates relative to their cost.

Section 3: Growth Planning for Your Cleaning Business

3.1 Scaling Your Operations

Expanding your cleaning business requires strategic planning:

- **Hire the Right Team**: As you grow, invest in skilled and reliable employees who share your values.
- **Expand Your Service Area**: Use market research to identify underserved neighborhoods or commercial zones.

- **Invest in Equipment**: Purchase high-efficiency machinery to handle larger jobs or specialized cleaning tasks.

3.2 Creating a Sustainable Growth Strategy

Avoid growing too quickly by focusing on sustainable practices:

- **Retain Existing Clients**: Focus on retention strategies like loyalty programs and excellent customer service.
- **Expand Gradually**: Test new markets or services on a small scale before full implementation.
- **Leverage Technology**: Use CRM systems to manage customer data and marketing automation to stay engaged with your clients.

3.3 Funding Your Growth

Scaling often requires external funding. Explore these options:

- **Small Business Loans**: Look for low-interest loans or government-backed programs.
- **Investor Funding**: Pitch your business plan to potential investors who understand your vision.
- **Reinvest Profits**: Allocate a percentage of your earnings toward growth initiatives.

Real-World Example: Growth Planning in Action

Case Study: Sparkle Pro Cleaners

- **Challenge**: Limited resources to expand beyond a single neighborhood.
- **Solution**:
    - Implemented cost-saving measures, reducing overhead by 15%.
    - Secured a small business loan to invest in marketing and equipment.

- o   Introduced premium services like eco-friendly cleaning for an additional revenue stream.
- **Outcome**:
  - o   Doubled the client base within 12 months.
  - o   Increased monthly revenue by 40%.

Conclusion

Financial management and growth planning form the backbone of any successful cleaning business. By mastering these skills, you can ensure stability and position yourself for long-term success. Use this chapter as a blueprint to build a financially sound, scalable business that thrives in the competitive cleaning service industry.

Chapter 11: Expanding and Scaling Your Business

Introduction

Expanding and scaling your cleaning business is a pivotal step in becoming an industry leader. Growth doesn't just mean acquiring more clients—it involves building a sustainable infrastructure, streamlining operations, and creating a strong brand that attracts customers consistently. This chapter focuses on strategies to expand your cleaning service, scale efficiently, and stand out in the highly competitive cleaning service industry. By the end of this chapter, you'll have a clear roadmap to take your business to the next level.

Section 1: Laying the Groundwork for Expansion

1.1 Evaluating Your Readiness to Expand

Before scaling, it's crucial to determine if your business is ready:

- **Financial Stability**: Ensure you have a consistent cash flow and healthy profit margins.
- **Operational Efficiency**: Assess if your current systems can handle increased demand.
- **Client Base**: Are you maxing out your capacity with current clients?

Checklist for Expansion:

- A proven track record of client satisfaction.
- Strong brand presence and local reputation.
- Access to capital for growth.

1.2 Identifying New Opportunities

Look for areas where demand exceeds supply:

- **Geographic Expansion**: Move into nearby neighborhoods or cities with untapped markets.
- **Service Diversification**: Offer specialized services like post-construction cleaning, industrial cleaning, or green cleaning.
- **Partnering with Local Businesses**: Establish contracts with property managers, hotels, or retail chains.

Pro Tip: Use market research tools like Google Trends or surveys to identify client needs in new areas.

1.3 Building Scalable Processes

Scalability is key to growth:

- **Standard Operating Procedures (SOPs)**: Document step-by-step workflows for every service.
- **Technology Adoption**: Invest in cleaning scheduling software, CRM systems, and automated invoicing tools.
- **Training Programs**: Create a standardized training program for onboarding new employees quickly and effectively.

Section 2: Effective Strategies for Scaling

2.1 Hiring and Retaining Top Talent

As you grow, your team becomes your most valuable asset:

- **Attracting Talent**: Offer competitive pay, benefits, and growth opportunities.

- **Retention Strategies**: Foster a positive work culture through employee recognition, flexible schedules, and clear career paths.
- **Leadership Development**: Promote from within and provide leadership training to key team members.

2.2 Marketing to New Markets

A robust marketing strategy ensures your services reach new clients:

- **Digital Marketing**:
    - Invest in search engine optimization (SEO) with keywords like "best cleaning services near me" or "affordable office cleaning."
    - Run targeted ads on social media platforms.
- **Referral Programs**: Encourage existing clients to refer your services in exchange for discounts or free services.
- **Local Outreach**: Distribute flyers, attend community events, and partner with local businesses to boost visibility.

2.3 Maintaining Quality While Scaling

Rapid growth often leads to compromised service quality, which must be avoided:

- **Regular Audits**: Conduct quality checks on services delivered by your team.
- **Client Feedback Loops**: Create channels where customers can easily share their opinions.
- **Continuous Training**: Ensure your team stays updated on the latest cleaning techniques and safety protocols.

Section 3: Sustaining Growth for the Long-Term

3.1 Building Strategic Partnerships

Collaboration can accelerate your growth:

- **Suppliers**: Negotiate better deals for bulk purchasing of cleaning supplies.
- **Corporate Contracts**: Partner with larger businesses that need recurring cleaning services.
- **Local Influencers**: Collaborate with influencers or bloggers in your area to showcase your services.

3.2 Leveraging Technology for Efficiency

Technology is a game-changer for scaling businesses:

- **Automation**: Use apps like Jobber or ServiceTitan to automate scheduling, dispatching, and billing.
- **Client Portals**: Create online portals where customers can book services, track appointments, and provide feedback.
- **Data Analytics**: Analyze client trends and preferences to refine your services.

3.3 Funding Your Expansion

Growth requires capital—know your options:

- **Small Business Loans**: Apply for SBA loans or other low-interest options.
- **Crowdfunding**: Share your vision with your community to gain financial support.
- **Angel Investors**: Pitch your expansion plans to investors looking for high-growth opportunities.

Real-World Example: Successful Scaling

Case Study: Fresh Shine Cleaning Co.

- **Challenge**: Limited to one neighborhood with stagnant growth.
- **Solution**:
    - Implemented a referral program that increased customer acquisition by 20%.

        - Adopted automated scheduling software, reducing manual errors.
        - Partnered with a local real estate agency to provide move-in/move-out cleaning services.
- **Outcome**:
    - Expanded to three new neighborhoods within a year.
    - Doubled annual revenue through strategic partnerships and service diversification.

Conclusion

Expanding and scaling your cleaning business is an exciting yet challenging process. By following the strategies outlined in this chapter, you can confidently navigate the complexities of growth while maintaining quality and customer satisfaction. Remember, successful scaling isn't about growing fast—it's about growing smart. With proper planning, the right team, and effective marketing, you can establish yourself as a leader in the cleaning service industry.

Chapter 12: Leveraging Technology in Your Cleaning Business

Introduction

In today's digital age, leveraging technology is no longer optional—it's essential for businesses aiming to thrive in competitive industries like cleaning services. Technology offers tools to streamline operations, enhance customer experiences, and boost profitability. This chapter explores innovative ways to incorporate technology into your cleaning business, providing a roadmap for beginners and established entrepreneurs alike.

Section 1: Embracing Digital Transformation in Cleaning Services

1.1 The Importance of Technology for Growth

Technology is not just a luxury but a powerful driver of growth and efficiency:

- **Automation**: Minimize repetitive tasks, saving time and reducing errors.
- **Enhanced Customer Experience**: Provide clients with seamless booking and service tracking.
- **Data-Driven Insights**: Use analytics to understand customer behavior and improve services.

1.2 Building a Tech-Savvy Foundation

Starting with the right tools ensures smooth integration:

- **Smart Devices**: Equip your team with smart vacuums, robotic floor cleaners, and IoT-enabled cleaning devices to enhance efficiency.
- **Digital Platforms**: Use apps for task management, payroll, and scheduling to keep operations organized.

- **Cloud Storage**: Store client records, employee details, and financial documents securely in cloud systems for easy access and safety.

1.3 Overcoming Resistance to Change

Transitioning to technology might feel overwhelming:

- **Employee Training**: Host workshops and training sessions to familiarize your team with new tools.
- **Customer Communication**: Inform clients about the added benefits of your tech-driven approach, such as eco-friendly solutions or faster response times.

Section 2: Technology for Business Operations

2.1 Automating Operations for Efficiency

Technology simplifies and streamlines daily operations:

- **Scheduling Software**: Platforms like Jobber or Housecall Pro help you manage bookings and assign tasks to employees.
- **Client Management Systems (CRMs)**: Keep track of client preferences, feedback, and recurring appointments.
- **Payment Automation**: Offer online payments through apps like Stripe or QuickBooks, making transactions hassle-free for clients.

2.2 Using Analytics to Drive Decisions

Analytics can transform your business approach:

- **Customer Data**: Track client preferences, service frequencies, and seasonal trends to adjust offerings.
- **Operational Metrics**: Monitor employee performance, cleaning times, and material usage to identify areas for improvement.

- **Profit Margins**: Use financial data to determine which services yield the best ROI.

2.3 Enhancing Team Productivity

Technology helps your cleaning team work smarter, not harder:

- **GPS Tracking**: Monitor employee locations and optimize travel routes for increased efficiency.
- **Mobile Communication Tools**: Use apps like Slack or WhatsApp for real-time updates and quick communication.
- **Smart Equipment**: Invest in energy-efficient, high-performance cleaning tools that reduce physical strain and time spent on tasks.

Section 3: Technology for Client Engagement

3.1 Digital Marketing to Boost Visibility

Maximize your reach with online marketing strategies:

- **Search Engine Optimization (SEO)**: Optimize your website with cleaning industry keywords like "eco-friendly house cleaning" or "office cleaning near me."
- **Social Media Platforms**: Share cleaning tips, before-and-after photos, and client testimonials on platforms like Instagram and Facebook.
- **Google My Business**: Ensure your business is listed with accurate contact details and positive reviews to attract local customers.

3.2 Online Booking Systems

Clients appreciate convenience:

- **Website Integration**: Add an online booking feature to your website.

- **Customizable Schedules**: Allow customers to select services, dates, and times that suit their needs.
- **Automatic Confirmations**: Send booking confirmations and reminders via email or SMS to reduce no-shows.

3.3 Building a Mobile App for Your Business

A dedicated app can revolutionize your client experience:

- **Real-Time Updates**: Provide notifications about service status or delays.
- **Loyalty Programs**: Reward repeat clients with discounts or free services.
- **Easy Feedback**: Allow clients to rate your services and provide feedback directly through the app.

Real-World Example: Tech Success in the Cleaning Industry

Case Study: CleanTech Pros

- **Challenge**: Inefficient manual processes and low client retention rates.
- **Solution**:
    - Adopted a CRM for managing client relationships and tracking service history.
    - Launched an app with online booking, live chat, and a loyalty rewards program.
    - Implemented eco-friendly robotic vacuums for residential services.
- **Outcome**:
    - Increased client retention by 35% through personalized services.
    - Reduced operational costs by 20% with automated scheduling.
    - Gained new clients through targeted social media ads.

Conclusion

Leveraging technology is a game-changing move for cleaning service businesses. By embracing digital tools and innovative solutions, you can streamline operations, enhance customer satisfaction, and achieve sustainable growth. Whether you're a new entrepreneur or looking to modernize your established business, the strategies in this chapter will position you as a leader in the cleaning industry.

Chapter 13: Navigating Challenges and Risks

Introduction

Running a cleaning business, like any other venture, comes with its own set of challenges and risks. From managing unpredictable customer demands to addressing operational hurdles and economic uncertainties, overcoming these obstacles is vital to building a resilient and successful company. This chapter equips cleaning business entrepreneurs with actionable strategies and insights to identify, mitigate, and manage risks effectively, ensuring long-term growth and stability in the industry.

Section 1: Identifying and Understanding Challenges

1.1 Common Operational Challenges in the Cleaning Industry

Recognizing the hurdles unique to cleaning services helps you prepare better:

- **Employee Turnover**: A common issue in service industries, leading to recruitment and training costs.
- **Seasonal Demand**: Peaks and troughs in cleaning service demand can affect cash flow.
- **Customer Expectations**: Clients expect high-quality, timely service—any misstep can lead to negative reviews.
- **Equipment Maintenance**: Frequent use of cleaning equipment can result in wear and tear, requiring ongoing maintenance.

1.2 Risk Assessment and Planning

A proactive approach to identifying risks minimizes surprises:

- **Financial Risks**: Unpaid invoices or unexpected expenses can disrupt cash flow.

- **Health and Safety Risks**: Cleaning chemicals and equipment can pose hazards to employees and clients.
- **Legal and Regulatory Compliance**: Adhering to local labor laws, insurance requirements, and safety standards is critical.
- **Reputation Management**: A single bad review or mishandled client issue can harm your business reputation.

1.3 Case Study: Recognizing Risks Early

A small cleaning business faced a sudden drop in clients due to poor service delivery during peak holiday seasons. By conducting a thorough review, they discovered inadequate staff training and miscommunication about service offerings were the root causes. Addressing these issues improved retention and restored client trust.

Section 2: Strategies to Mitigate Risks

2.1 Employee Retention and Training

Investing in your team can help reduce turnover and improve service quality:

- **Competitive Compensation**: Offer fair wages and bonuses for consistent performers.
- **Regular Training Programs**: Equip your staff with the latest cleaning techniques and customer service skills.
- **Recognition Programs**: Acknowledge hard work with incentives, awards, or public recognition.

2.2 Financial Planning and Stability

Strong financial practices are key to weathering economic uncertainty:

- **Cash Flow Management**: Maintain an emergency fund to handle unforeseen expenses.
- **Invoice Automation**: Use billing software to ensure timely payments and reduce missed invoices.

- **Diversified Income Streams**: Offer additional services, such as carpet cleaning or window washing, to maintain steady income year-round.

2.3 Legal Compliance and Safety Standards

Protect your business and employees by staying compliant:

- **Insurance Coverage**: Secure liability, property, and workers' compensation insurance.
- **Safety Training**: Educate employees on the safe use of chemicals and equipment.
- **Regulatory Updates**: Stay informed about changes in labor laws, tax regulations, and environmental guidelines.

Section 3: Building Resilience in a Competitive Market

3.1 Proactive Customer Engagement

Strong client relationships can protect your business from market fluctuations:

- **Loyalty Programs**: Reward regular clients with discounts, free add-ons, or exclusive offers.
- **Feedback Mechanisms**: Regularly seek and implement client suggestions to improve services.
- **Crisis Communication**: Have a plan to address service issues or negative reviews swiftly and professionally.

3.2 Leveraging Technology to Manage Risks

Digital tools can simplify risk management and improve efficiency:

- **CRM Software**: Track client preferences, billing, and service histories to ensure consistent quality.
- **Digital Marketing**: Use targeted campaigns to attract new clients during slow periods.

- **Maintenance Scheduling**: Automate reminders for servicing or replacing equipment.

3.3 Adapting to Market Changes

Flexibility is crucial for long-term success:

- **Eco-Friendly Services**: Incorporate green cleaning products to appeal to environmentally-conscious clients.
- **Flexible Offerings**: Adjust service packages based on seasonal trends or customer needs.
- **Competitive Analysis**: Monitor competitors' strategies to stay ahead in the market.

Real-World Example: Thriving Amid Challenges

Case Study: GreenClean Solutions

- **Problem**: Employee turnover and increasing equipment maintenance costs were affecting profits.
- **Solution**:
    - Implemented an employee retention program with performance-based bonuses.
    - Upgraded to durable, eco-friendly cleaning tools with lower maintenance requirements.
    - Launched a digital booking platform to improve client convenience and satisfaction.
- **Outcome**:
    - Reduced turnover by 25% and improved client satisfaction scores by 40%.
    - Achieved a 15% increase in revenue within a year.

Conclusion

Challenges and risks are inevitable in the cleaning business, but with the right strategies and mindset, they can be transformed into opportunities for growth. By identifying potential risks early, investing in your team, and leveraging technology, you can create a resilient business that stands out in the competitive cleaning industry.

Chapter 14: Case Studies and Real-World Success Stories

Introduction

Nothing inspires and teaches better than real-world examples of success. This chapter dives deep into the journeys of cleaning business entrepreneurs who overcame challenges, implemented innovative strategies, and achieved remarkable milestones in the cleaning service industry. By learning from these case studies, you will gain actionable insights, motivational lessons, and proven tactics that you can adapt and implement in your own cleaning business.

Section 1: Transformative Success Stories

1.1 From Solo Cleaner to Multi-Location Empire

Case Study: Sparkling Spaces Cleaning Services

- **Overview**: A single mother, Maria Lopez, started her cleaning business from her garage with minimal resources. Over a decade, she grew Sparkling Spaces into a multi-location franchise serving both residential and commercial clients.
- **Key Challenges**:
    - Lack of initial funding.
    - Building a reliable customer base.
    - Scaling operations while maintaining quality.
- **Strategies for Success**:
    - **Personalized Service**: Maria focused on building relationships with clients, offering tailored cleaning plans to fit their unique needs.
    - **Referral Program**: She introduced a referral program, offering discounts to customers who brought in new business.
    - **Technology Integration**: Sparkling Spaces adopted a booking app early on, streamlining scheduling and payment processes.
- **Outcome**: Sparkling Spaces grew from one location to 15 within 10 years, generating annual revenue of over $5 million.

1.2 Achieving Niche Market Dominance

Case Study: EcoClean Solutions

- **Overview**: Tom Nguyen identified a gap in the market for environmentally friendly cleaning services in urban areas.
- **Key Challenges**:
    - Educating customers about the benefits of eco-friendly cleaning.
    - Sourcing cost-effective, sustainable cleaning supplies.
- **Strategies for Success**:
    - **Marketing Campaigns**: Tom launched a targeted marketing campaign, highlighting the health and environmental benefits of using green products.
    - **Strategic Partnerships**: He collaborated with local suppliers to secure bulk discounts on eco-friendly materials.
    - **Certifications**: EcoClean obtained certifications from green organizations, boosting credibility and trust.
- **Outcome**: Within three years, EcoClean became the go-to service for eco-conscious homeowners, achieving 150% growth in clientele annually.

Section 2: Overcoming Challenges to Build Resilience

2.1 Bouncing Back from a Financial Crisis

Case Study: Shiny Spot Cleaners

- **Overview**: A family-owned cleaning business faced bankruptcy after losing two major commercial contracts.
- **Key Challenges**:
    - Sudden revenue drop.
    - High operational costs.
- **Strategies for Recovery**:

- - **Diversified Services**: The company diversified into post-construction cleaning and move-in/move-out services.
  - **Cost-Cutting Measures**: Management renegotiated vendor contracts and streamlined operations.
  - **Digital Marketing**: They utilized social media platforms and local SEO to reach new clients.
- **Outcome**: Shiny Spot Cleaners not only survived but expanded its client base by 40% within two years.

2.2 Handling Customer Retention Issues

Case Study: Pristine Cleaning Pros

- **Overview**: A medium-sized cleaning business faced a decline in repeat customers due to inconsistent service quality.
- **Key Challenges**:
  - High employee turnover.
  - Poor customer feedback.
- **Strategies for Improvement**:
  - **Employee Training**: Implemented a rigorous onboarding and training program.
  - **Customer Feedback Systems**: Introduced surveys after every cleaning session to gather client insights.
  - **Loyalty Rewards**: Offered discounts and bonuses for long-term customers.
- **Outcome**: The business regained 75% of its lost customers and significantly improved its reputation in the market.

Section 3: Scaling and Innovating

3.1 Leveraging Franchising for Expansion

Case Study: Supreme Shine Cleaning Co.

- **Overview**: Supreme Shine transitioned from a small local business to a franchise model, with over 50 locations across the country.

- **Key Challenges**:
    - Maintaining quality control across locations.
    - Recruiting franchisees who aligned with company values.
- **Strategies for Growth**:
    - **Comprehensive Training Programs**: Franchisees underwent intensive training to ensure service consistency.
    - **Franchisee Support Systems**: Supreme Shine provided marketing, HR, and operational support to franchisees.
    - **Innovative Marketing**: The company launched creative campaigns, including video testimonials from satisfied customers.
- **Outcome**: Supreme Shine became one of the most recognized cleaning service brands, generating $20 million in annual revenue.

3.2 Innovation in Technology Adoption

Case Study: RoboClean Services

- **Overview**: RoboClean leveraged automation and AI-driven cleaning solutions to revolutionize commercial cleaning.
- **Key Challenges**:
    - High initial investment.
    - Resistance from traditional clients.
- **Strategies for Innovation**:
    - **Client Demonstrations**: Hosted live demos showcasing the efficiency and effectiveness of robotic cleaners.
    - **Cost-Benefit Analysis**: Highlighted long-term cost savings to clients.
    - **Hybrid Model**: Combined robotic cleaning with human oversight to ensure quality.
- **Outcome**: RoboClean became an industry pioneer, attracting high-profile corporate clients and earning awards for innovation.

Conclusion

These success stories highlight the endless possibilities for growth and innovation in the cleaning industry. Whether you are starting small or scaling up, these real-world examples provide a roadmap to navigate challenges, implement effective strategies, and achieve unparalleled success.

Chapter 15: Sustained Success and Future Trends

Introduction

Success in the cleaning business industry is not just about achieving growth but also sustaining it over the long term. As an entrepreneur, understanding future trends, adapting to market shifts, and continually improving your services are essential to staying competitive. This chapter will provide actionable strategies for maintaining long-term success while preparing for and capitalizing on emerging trends in the cleaning service industry.

Section 1: Building a Sustainable Cleaning Business

1.1 Establishing a Customer-Centric Business Model

Customers are the foundation of your business. Building a loyal customer base is key to sustained success.

- **Key Strategies**:
    - **Focus on Customer Retention**: Create loyalty programs offering discounts, free services, or exclusive benefits for repeat customers.
    - **Personalized Experiences**: Use customer data to tailor cleaning services to individual needs. For example, offer deep-cleaning packages based on seasonal requirements.
    - **Regular Feedback Loops**: Implement surveys or follow-ups after each service to address concerns and improve.

1.2 Operational Efficiency

Efficiency not only reduces costs but also enhances service quality.

- **Steps to Improve Efficiency**:

- o **Adopt Technology**: Use scheduling software, route optimization tools, and automated reminders to streamline operations.
- o **Employee Productivity**: Train staff in time management and ensure they have the right tools for their job.
- o **Minimize Wastage**: Implement sustainable practices, such as using refillable cleaning products and energy-efficient equipment.

1.3 Financial Health

A financially sound business can weather economic downturns.

- **Key Practices**:
    - o **Diversified Revenue Streams**: Explore niche markets such as post-construction cleaning, event cleaning, or medical facility cleaning.
    - o **Regular Audits**: Monitor expenses and identify areas for cost savings.
    - o **Build Reserves**: Save a percentage of profits for emergencies or future investments.

Section 2: Adapting to Market Changes

2.1 The Growing Demand for Green Cleaning

Sustainability is more than a buzzword; it's a critical factor in consumer decision-making.

- **How to Adapt**:
    - o Offer eco-friendly cleaning packages using biodegradable and non-toxic products.

- Highlight certifications and eco-friendly initiatives in marketing materials.
- Partner with suppliers who share your commitment to sustainability.

2.2 Technology as a Game Changer

From automation to data analytics, technology is reshaping the cleaning industry.

- **Key Innovations**:
    - **Robotic Cleaning**: Invest in automated vacuum cleaners or floor scrubbers to improve efficiency.
    - **Customer Relationship Management (CRM)**: Use CRM tools to manage customer interactions, track leads, and personalize marketing efforts.
    - **AI and IoT**: Explore AI-powered tools for predictive maintenance and IoT devices for remote monitoring of cleaning operations.

2.3 Demographic Shifts and Urbanization

As cities grow, so does the demand for reliable cleaning services.

- **Opportunities**:
    - Target densely populated areas with specialized services such as high-rise window cleaning or co-working space maintenance.
    - Appeal to younger demographics with flexible, on-demand cleaning options.

Section 3: Preparing for the Future

3.1 Emerging Trends to Watch

The cleaning industry is constantly evolving, and staying ahead of the curve is essential.

- **Automation and AI**: Expect increased adoption of robots for repetitive cleaning tasks.
- **Health-Centric Cleaning**: The pandemic has heightened awareness of cleanliness. Offer services focused on disinfection and sanitization.
- **Subscription Models**: Introduce subscription-based cleaning plans for consistent revenue and customer retention.

3.2 Scaling Responsibly

Growth is exciting, but it must be sustainable.

- **Controlled Expansion**: Open new locations only after ensuring your existing operations are stable.
- **Franchise Opportunities**: If successful, consider franchising your model to expand while sharing responsibilities.
- **Cultural Alignment**: Ensure all new hires and branches uphold the values and service quality your brand represents.

3.3 The Role of Branding and Marketing

A strong brand can position you as a leader in the cleaning industry.

- **Brand Storytelling**: Share your journey and values through blogs, social media, and promotional materials.
- **Engaging Content**: Produce cleaning tips, behind-the-scenes videos, or customer testimonials to engage your audience.
- **Partnerships**: Collaborate with local influencers or businesses to boost your visibility.

Conclusion

Sustained success in the cleaning industry is built on adaptability, customer focus, and staying ahead of market trends. By implementing the strategies in this chapter, you will not only maintain your current success but also prepare your business for future opportunities, ensuring longevity in a competitive market.

General Summary and Conclusion

Summary

Blueprint for Cleaning Business Success: Crafting the Perfect Plan is a comprehensive, actionable guide designed to help aspiring entrepreneurs and seasoned professionals excel in the cleaning service industry. Each chapter in this book provides in-depth insights, practical strategies, and real-world examples, making it a must-have resource for navigating every aspect of building and growing a cleaning business.

The book begins with the **foundational steps** of starting a cleaning business, focusing on planning, goal-setting, and creating a strong business framework. It walks readers through **branding and marketing strategies**, emphasizing the importance of customer relationships and standing out in a competitive market. The emphasis on financial management ensures that readers are equipped to handle budgets, profits, and growth effectively, while actionable steps for expanding, scaling, and leveraging technology provide a roadmap for long-term success.

Critical challenges such as employee management, sustainability, and navigating industry risks are addressed with clarity, offering tools and solutions for overcoming obstacles. The inclusion of **case studies and real-world success stories** highlights practical examples and inspires readers to apply their learnings to their own ventures. Finally, the book concludes with a forward-looking discussion on **sustained success and future trends**, ensuring entrepreneurs stay ahead in an ever-evolving industry.

Conclusion

The cleaning service industry is not just a business opportunity—it's a dynamic and growing field with immense potential for those willing to put in the work and learn from experts. ***Blueprint for Cleaning Business Success: Crafting the Perfect Plan*** provides a step-by-step guide to mastering every element of the cleaning business, from inception to scaling and beyond.

Whether you're starting small or aiming for industry dominance, this book equips you with the tools, strategies, and inspiration to achieve your goals. The emphasis on innovation, adaptability, and customer-centric service ensures you're not just running a business but creating a lasting legacy.

This book isn't just a resource—it's a partner in your entrepreneurial journey, ensuring your cleaning business becomes not only profitable but also a benchmark for excellence in the industry. Now, it's time to take action, implement these strategies, and build your path to success. Your future in the cleaning service industry starts here!

About the Author

Jerry Ikome Nganje, the mastermind behind ***Blueprint for Cleaning Business Success: Crafting the Perfect Plan***, is an inspiring figure in the cleaning service industry. Drawing from his profound experiences, boundless passion, and unshakable faith, Jerry has become a beacon of hope and guidance for entrepreneurs, especially those embarking on their first business journey. His story is a testament to resilience, determination, and the belief that anyone can build something extraordinary when they trust the process and put it in God's hands.

Jerry's entrepreneurial journey is deeply rooted in his unwavering commitment to helping others succeed. Recognized as an "industry plant," Jerry's expertise feels divinely orchestrated, offering a blend of practical insights and heartfelt wisdom. He doesn't just share theories; he provides actionable steps derived from real-world experience, ensuring every reader feels empowered and equipped to chase their dreams.

Through this book, Jerry's mission is clear: to make the cleaning service industry accessible to everyone, no matter their background or starting point. His writing is infused with humility, making it easy for readers to connect with him as a mentor and fellow entrepreneur. Jerry knows the challenges and fears of starting a business—because he's been there. Yet, he also knows the immense satisfaction of turning those challenges into stepping stones toward greatness.

Blueprint for Cleaning Business Success isn't just a book for Jerry; it's a calling. It represents his desire to guide others toward creating businesses that not only thrive financially but also leave a lasting impact on clients, employees, and communities. For Jerry, success isn't about personal accolades—it's about giving glory to God and lifting others up along the way.

In Jerry's own words:
"I'm not just here to share strategies; I'm here to walk this journey with you. Together, with hard work and God's guidance, we can build something extraordinary. The path may not always be easy, but I promise you, it's worth it."

Jerry Ikome Nganje is not just an author—he's a builder of dreams, a cultivator of success, and a steadfast believer in the potential of every aspiring entrepreneur. If you're ready to transform your ideas into reality, Jerry's story and guidance will light your way.

NOTES

www.ingramcontent.com/pod-product-compliance
Lightning Source LLC
Chambersburg PA
CBHW071107240526
45469CB00006BD/2363